101 Things To Do With Ground Beef

101 Things To Do With Ground Beef

BY
STEPHANIE ASHCRAFT
AND JANET EYRING

GIBBS SMITH
Gibbs Smith, Publisher
SALT LAKE CITY

First Edition
10 09 08 07 06 20 19 18 17 16 15 14 13 12 11 10 9 8 7 6 5 4 3 2 1

Published by
Gibbs Smith, Publisher
P.O. Box 667
Layton, Utah 84041

Orders: 1.800.748.5439
www.gibbs-smith.com

Designed by Kurt Wahlner
Printed and bound in Korea

Library of Congress Cataloging-in-Publication Data

Ashcraft, Stephanie.

101 things to do with ground beef / Stephanie Ashcraft and Janet Eyring.—1st ed.

p. cm.

ISBN 1-4236-0061-4

1. Cookery (Beef) I. Title: One hundred and one things to do with ground beef. II. Title: One hundred one things to do with ground beef. III. Eyring, Janet. IV. Title.

TX749.5.B43A84 2006
641.6'62—dc22

2006007316

To my sister, Katrina. Thank you for
all the support and encouragement you
have always given me. I love you.
—S.A.

To the David and Kandis Broadhead
family for donating countless pounds of
ground beef. I am extremely grateful.
—J.E.

CONTENTS

Meat Loaf

Main Dishes

Family Favorites

HELPFUL HINTS

1. Ground beef should be always be bright red. Avoid buying meat with brown or gray patches and always check the sell-by date on the package.

2. Ground beef packages are labeled with a percentage ratio of lean meat to fat. The higher number on the package indicates the lean percentage. For example, if a package is labeled 93/7, it is 93 percent lean. We use 85 to 93 percent lean ground beef in the majority of our recipes. The most leanest require little or no draining when cooked.

3. Ground beef that is 75 percent lean can be cooked, drained, and best used in sides, soups, sloppy joes, barbequed sandwiches, and pizzas.

4. Ground beef that is 85 percent lean or higher can be used for meat loaves, meatballs, and hamburgers. Ground chuck may also be used.

5. Ground beef that is 93 percent lean is best used for low-fat dishes, such as casseroles or main dishes. Ground round or ground sirloin also work well.

6. Refrigerated ground beef should be used within 1 to 2 days of purchase. Ground beef can be stored in the freezer for up to 3 months if removed from its original package and wrapped in freezer paper or stored in freezer bags.

7. One of the best ways to avoid freezer burn is to use a vacuum food sealer to remove oxygen before freezing meat.

8. Buy ground beef in bulk. Separate into 1-pound increments and freeze for future use in freezer bags.

9. To thaw frozen ground beef, place meat in the refrigerator the night before. The microwave can be used to defrost the frozen ground beef as well. Never allow frozen meat to thaw at room temperature.

10. Never eat raw ground beef. Make sure it is cooked until no longer pink or the internal temperature reaches 160 degrees.

11. To drain excess fat from meat, cook meat until brown. With spatula push meat to one side of pan allowing excess fat to pool at opposite end of pan. Remove fat with a soup spoon and discard.

12. Avoid refreezing meat that has previously been frozen and thawed.

13. Low fat or low sodium products may be used in all recipes.

Appetizers

BACON-WRAPPED PATTIES

1 pound	**ground beef**
1/2 cup	**grated sharp cheddar cheese**
1 tablespoon	**lemon juice**
1/2 cup	**chopped green bell pepper**
2 tablespoons	**chopped pimientos**
1 cup	**seasoned breadcrumbs**
1 egg	**slightly beaten**
8 slices	**uncooked bacon**

Preheat oven to 375 degrees.

In a bowl, combine all ingredients except bacon. Mix well. Shape into 8 balls. With a glass cup, flatten balls until 1 1/2 inches thick. Wrap a slice of bacon around the outer edge of each patty and then secure with a toothpick. Bake 40–45 minutes, or until internal temperature reaches 165 degrees. Makes 8 servings.

BEEFED-UP BEAN DIP

1 pound	**ground beef**
1 can (15 ounces)	**refried beans**
8 ounces	**Velveeta cheese,** cubed
2 cans (8 ounces each)	**tomato sauce**
1 can (4 ounces)	**chopped green chiles**, drained
	tortilla chips

In a frying pan, brown ground beef until meat is no longer pink. Drain if necessary. Add beans, cheese, and tomato sauce to cooked beef. Stir until cheese melts. Add green chiles. Serve with tortilla chips. Makes 6–8 servings.

*This recipe can be placed in a slow cooker on low heat and served at a party.

BLACK BEAN NACHOS

1 pound **ground beef**
1 **medium onion**, chopped
1 **green bell pepper**, seeded and chopped
1 can (15.25 ounces) **black beans,** rinsed and drained
1 can (14.5 ounces) **sliced stewed tomatoes,** with liquid
1 envelope **taco seasoning**
1 bag (10 ounces or larger) **tortilla chips**
grated cheddar or Monterey Jack cheese
sliced black olives (optional)
sour cream (optional)

In a frying pan, brown ground beef, onion, and bell pepper until meat is no longer pink. Drain if necessary. Stir in beans, tomatoes, and taco seasoning. Simmer over low heat for 10 minutes.

Spoon meat mixture over individual servings of tortilla chips. Sprinkle cheese over top. Garnish with sliced black olives and sour cream if desired. Makes 8–10 servings.

VARIATION: Meat filling can also be served burrito style in warm soft flour tortillas.

BEEF WONTONS

1/2 pound	**ground beef**
2 tablespoons	**soy sauce**
2 teaspoons	**dried minced onion**
1/2 teaspoon	**ginger**
1/4 teaspoon	**salt**
1 package (12 ounces)	**square wonton wrappers**
	vegetable or canola oil

Sauce:

1/4 cup	**soy sauce**
1/3 cup	**vinegar**
2/3 cup	**water**
3/4 cup	**sugar**
2 tablespoons	**cornstarch**

In a frying pan, brown ground beef until meat is no longer pink. Drain if necessary. Stir in soy sauce, onion, ginger, and salt.

Spoon a heaping 1/2 teaspoon beef mixture onto each wonton wrapper. Fold wrapper over meat mixture and seal edges with water. Fry, turning once, in hot oil for 2 minutes until lightly golden.

In a saucepan, combine all sauce ingredients. Cook over low heat, stirring constantly until sauce thickens. Serve wontons with sauce on the side. Makes 48 wontons.

TACO LAYER DIP

1 pound	**ground beef**
1 envelope	**taco seasoning,** divided
1 package (8 ounces)	**cream cheese**
1/2 cup	**sour cream**
2 tablespoons	**mayonnaise**
1	**small onion,** chopped
1 1/2 cups	**grated cheddar cheese**
1 bag (10 ounces)	**chopped lettuce**
1	**large tomato,** chopped
	tortilla chips
	sliced black olives (optional)

In a frying pan, brown ground beef until meat is no longer pink. Drain if necessary. Season meat with half the taco seasoning. Set aside to cool.

In a bowl, combine cream cheese, sour cream, mayonnaise, remaining taco seasoning, and onion. Spread mixture into bottom of a 9 x 13-inch pan. Sprinkle cooled meat mixture over top. Refrigerate until ready to serve.

Immediately before serving, sprinkle cheese, lettuce, and tomato over meat layer. Serve with tortilla chips. Garnish with sliced olives if desired. Makes 10–12 servings.

BARBEQUE TACO PLATTER

1 pound	**ground beef**
1/2 cup	**water**
1 envelope	**taco seasoning**
2 packages (8 ounces each)	**cream cheese,** softened
1/3 cup	**milk**
1 can (4 ounces)	**chopped green chiles**
1	**large tomato,** chopped
1/2 cup	**chopped green onions**
2 cups	**shredded lettuce**
3/4 cup	**honey barbeque sauce**
1 1/2 cups	**grated cheddar cheese**
1 bag (10 ounces)	**tortilla chips**

In a frying pan, brown ground beef until meat is no longer pink. Drain if necessary. Return meat to pan and add water and taco seasoning. Simmer for 5 minutes.

In a medium bowl, combine cream cheese and milk. Spread cream cheese mixture on a 12-inch pizza pan. Top with cooked beef. Sprinkle chiles, tomato, and green onions over the meat mixture. Drizzle barbeque sauce over the top and sprinkle with lettuce and cheese. Serve with tortilla chips. Makes 8–10 servings.

PARTY-READY MEAT ON RYE

1 pound **ground beef**
12 ounces **ground sausage**
1 package (16 ounces) **Velveeta cheese,** cubed
2 teaspoons **Italian seasoning**
1 teaspoon **garlic salt**
1 teaspoon **pepper**
1 loaf (16 ounces) **cocktail rye bread,** precut in 1/4-inch slices

In a frying pan, brown ground beef and sausage until no longer pink. Drain if necessary. Stir in cheese and seasonings. Cook over low heat, stirring occasionally until cheese is melted. Spread meat mixture onto rye slices and then place slices onto two large baking sheets. Cover with plastic wrap. Freeze for 1 hour. Carefully place in freezer bags until ready to use.

To bake, preheat oven to 350 degrees. Place frozen appetizers on baking sheet. Bake for 15–20 minutes, or until bread is toasted and meat is hot. Makes 43–45 appetizers.

BAKED MEATBALLS

1 pound **ground beef**
1/2 pound **ground sausage**
3/4 cup **applesauce**
1 cup **fine dry breadcrumbs**
1 teaspoon **salt**
1/4 teaspoon **pepper**
1 can (10.75 ounces) **tomato soup,** condensed
1/4 cup **water**

Preheat oven to 375 degrees.

In a large bowl, combine ground beef, sausage, applesauce, bread-crumbs, salt, and pepper. Shape into 24 meatballs. Place meatballs in a 2-quart baking dish.

In a small bowl, blend tomato soup and water. Pour over meatballs, cover and bake 1 hour, or until meatballs are no longer pink. Makes 8 servings.

GREAT-GRANDMA STOWELL'S MEATBALLS

1 envelope	**dry onion soup mix**
2 cups	**water**
1	**egg,** slightly beaten
1/2 cup	**milk**
3/4 cup	**quick oats**
1 pound	**ground beef**
1 teaspoon	**salt**
1/4 teaspoon	**pepper**

In a bowl, combine soup mix and water. Let stand.

In a separate bowl, mix egg, milk, and oats. Stir in ground beef, salt, and pepper. Shape into 1-inch balls. Place in a large frying pan to brown. After browned, pour onion soup mixture over meatballs. Cover and simmer over low heat for 20 minutes. Makes 4–6 servings.

CORN FLAKE MEATBALLS

1 pound **ground beef**
1 **egg,** beaten
1/4 cup **applesauce**
1/2 cup **crushed corn flakes**
1 small **onion,** chopped
1/2 teaspoon **salt**
1/4 teaspoon **pepper**
1/4 teaspoon **garlic salt**
1 can (8 ounces) **tomato sauce**

Preheat oven to 350 degrees.

In a large bowl, combine all ingredients except tomato sauce. Shape mixture into 16 meatballs. Place meatballs into a greased 9 x 13-inch pan. Pour tomato sauce over the top. Bake for 1 hour. Makes 4–6 servings.

HAWAIIAN MEATBALLS

1 pound **ground beef**
2/3 cup **saltine cracker crumbs**
1/2 cup **minced onion**
1 **egg,** slightly beaten
1 teaspoon **salt**
1/2 teaspoon **ginger**
1/4 cup **milk**

Sauce:

2 tablespoons **cornstarch**
2/3 cup **brown sugar**
1/2 cup **white vinegar**
2 tablespoons **low-sodium soy sauce**
1 can (20 ounces) **crushed pineapple,** juice reserved

Preheat oven to 400 degrees.

In a bowl, combine ground beef, cracker crumbs, onion, egg, salt, ginger, and milk. Shape into 16 meatballs. Bake on an ungreased baking sheet for 45 minutes. Remove pan from oven and place meatballs on paper towels to drain.

Meanwhile, in a saucepan, combine cornstarch, brown sugar, vinegar, soy sauce, and pineapple juice over medium-low heat until thick, stirring constantly. Boil 1 minute. Add meatballs and pineapple and heat through. Makes 4–6 servings.

PORCUPINE MEATBALLS

1 can (10.75 ounces) **tomato soup,** condensed and divided
1 pound **ground beef**
1 cup **uncooked instant rice**
1 **egg,** beaten
1/4 **medium onion,** chopped
1 teaspoon **salt**
1/2 teaspoon **pepper**
3/4 cup **water**
1 teaspoon **yellow mustard**
2 to 3 **cloves garlic,** minced

In a large bowl, combine 1/4 cup soup, ground beef, rice, egg, onion, salt, and pepper. Shape into 16 meatballs.

In a frying pan, brown meatballs about 7–10 minutes. Drain excess grease if necessary.

In a separate bowl, mix remaining soup, water, mustard, and garlic. Pour mixture over meatballs. Cover and simmer over low heat 20 minutes or until done, stirring occasionally. Makes 4 servings.

EGG ROLLS

2 to 3	**cloves garlic,** minced
1	**small onion,** diced
1 pound	**ground beef**
4	**medium carrots,** shredded
1/2	**head cabbage,** shredded
1 package (25 count)	**egg roll wrappers**
	oil

In a frying pan, saute garlic and onion until onion is transparent. Add ground beef; brown and drain well. Add carrots, cover and cook for 1–2 minutes. Add cabbage, cover and cook for 1–2 minutes more. Drain excess water and let mixture cool. Spoon about 2 tablespoons meat mixture onto each egg roll wrapper. Follow package directions on how to fold egg roll. Deep fry in oil until golden brown. Makes 25 egg rolls.

Sides & Soups

BEEFED-UP PORK AND BEANS

1 pound	**ground beef**
4 cans (16 ounces each)	**pork and beans**
2 tablespoons	**mustard**
1 cup	**ketchup**
1/2 cup	**brown sugar**
2 tablespoons	**Worcestershire sauce**
1	**medium onion**, chopped

Preheat oven to 400 degrees.

In a frying pan, brown ground beef until no longer pink. Drain if necessary. Combine meat with all remaining ingredients in a greased 3- to 4-quart baking dish. Bake 40–45 minutes, or until bubbly. Makes 8–10 servings.

BACON CALICO BEANS

1/2 pound **bacon**
1/2 pound **ground beef**
1 medium **onion,** chopped
1 can (16 ounces) **garbanzo beans,** drained
1 can (16 ounces) **kidney beans,** drained
1 can (16 ounces) **lima beans,** drained
3 cans (16 ounces each) **pork and beans**
1/2 cup **ketchup**
3/4 cup **brown sugar**
2 tablespoons **yellow mustard**
2 teaspoons **white vinegar**
1/2 teaspoon **salt**

In a large frying pan, cook bacon, ground beef, and onion until meat is no longer pink. Drain if necessary. Add remaining ingredients into frying pan. Heat through and serve. Makes 8–10 servings.

HUNGRY BOY BEANS

1 pound	**ground beef**
1 medium	**onion,** chopped
1 cup	**chopped green bell pepper**
1 can (8 ounces)	**tomato sauce**
1 cup	**water**
1 can (16 ounces)	**kidney beans**
1 can (16 ounces)	**pork and beans**
1 can (16 ounces)	**Great Northern white beans**

In a frying pan, brown ground beef with onion and bell pepper until meat is no longer pink and onion is translucent. Drain if necessary. Add remaining ingredients and simmer over low heat 1 hour. Makes 6–8 servings.

MEATBALL AND MINI STARS SOUP

1 bag (32 ounces)	**frozen fully-cooked meatballs***
2 to 3	**cloves garlic,** minced
1/2 cup	**chopped onion**
1/2 cup	**diced celery**
2 tablespoons	**olive oil**
6 cups	**chicken broth**
1 1/2 cups	**crushed tomatoes**
1 teaspoon	**Italian seasoning**
1/2 teaspoon	**salt**
1/4 teaspoon	**pepper**
1/2 cup	**dry mini star pasta**

In a frying pan, cook meatballs over medium-low heat 8–10 minutes. Set aside.

In a large stockpot, saute garlic, onion, and celery in oil until onion is transparent. Add meatballs, chicken broth, tomatoes, Italian seasoning, salt, and pepper. Bring to a simmer and add star pasta. Simmer an additional 2–4 minutes, or until pasta is done. Makes 4–6 servings.

*Can be found in the frozen meat section. Your favorite meatball recipe may be substituted.

HOTTER-THAN-HOT CHILI WITH BEANS

2 medium	**onions,** chopped
2 to 3	**garlic cloves,** minced
6 teaspoons	**chili powder**
2 tablespoons	**vegetable oil**
2 pounds	**ground beef**
1 1/2 to 2 teaspoons	**salt**
3 cups	**water**
3 cans (16 ounces each)	**kidney beans,** undrained
2 teaspoons	**ground cumin**

In a frying pan, saute onions and garlic with chili powder in oil until onions are transparent. Drain and set aside.

In the same frying pan, brown ground beef with salt until meat is no longer pink. Return onions to frying pan and add water. Simmer 40–45 minutes. Add kidney beans and cumin and simmer 45–60 minutes. Makes 8 servings.

STUFFED BELL PEPPER SOUP

1 pound	**ground beef**
1	**green bell pepper,** seeded and chopped
1 can (15 ounces)	**tomato sauce**
2 cups	**water**
1 can (14.5 ounces)	**Italian-style diced tomatoes,** with liquid
1	**beef bouillon cube**
1/2 teaspoon	**salt**
1/2 teaspoon	**black pepper**
1 1/2 teaspoons	**soy sauce**
1 1/2 cups	**cooked white rice**

In a frying pan, brown ground beef until no longer pink. Drain if necessary. Stir in bell pepper, tomato sauce, water, tomatoes, bouillon, salt, pepper, and soy sauce. Reduce heat to low, cover and simmer for 30–45 minutes. Stir in rice and heat 5 minutes more. Makes 6–8 servings.

WINTER CHILI

1 1/2 to 2 pounds **ground beef,** browned and drained
1 can (29 ounces) **tomato sauce**
1 can (15 ounces) **kidney beans,** with liquid
3 cans (15 ounces each) **pinto beans,** with liquid
1 **medium onion,** diced
1 can (4 ounces) **chopped green chiles**
1 can (29 ounces) **petite diced tomatoes,** with liquid
2 teaspoons **cumin**
3 tablespoons **chili powder**
1 teaspoon **pepper**
1 1/2 teaspoons **salt**
2 cups **water**

In a large stockpot, combine all ingredients and simmer over low heat 1 hour, stirring occasionally. Makes 12–15 servings.

AUTUMN POTLUCK SOUP

3 tablespoons	**butter or margarine**
1	**medium onion,** chopped
1 1/2 to 2 pounds	**ground beef**
3 cans (14.5 ounces each)	**beef broth**
3 cups	**water**
1 can (29 ounces)	**diced tomatoes,** with liquid
4	**carrots,** sliced
2	**ribs celery plus leaves,** chopped
1 cup	**uncooked shell macaroni**
1 teaspoon	**parsley**
1/2 teaspoon	**thyme**
1 teaspoon	**salt**
1/2 teaspoon	**pepper**

In a stockpot, saute butter and onion until onion is transparent. Remove onion and set aside.

In the same pan, brown ground beef until meat is no longer pink. Drain well. Return onion, and add remaining ingredients. Bring to a boil over medium-high heat. Reduce heat and simmer for 15–20 minutes, or until macaroni is done. Makes 4–6 servings.

FEED THE POSSE STEW

1 pound **ground beef,** browned and drained
1 can (15 ounces) **whole kernel corn,** with liquid
1 can (15 ounces) **hominy**
1 can (15 ounces) **ranch beans,** with liquid
1 can (4 ounces) **chopped green chiles**
1 **medium onion,** chopped
1 can (29 ounces) **stewed tomatoes,** with liquid
2 packages (1 ounce each) **brown gravy mix**

In a large stockpot, combine ground beef, corn, hominy, beans, chiles, and onion.

In a blender, combine stewed tomatoes and gravy mixes. Pulse until coarsely chopped. Pour tomato mixture into stockpot. Cover and simmer over low heat 1 hour, stirring occasionally. Makes 4–6 servings.

GRANDMA'S TACO SOUP

1 pound	**ground beef**
1	**medium onion,** chopped
1 can (14.5 ounces)	**diced tomatoes,** with liquid
1 can (8 ounces)	**tomato sauce**
1 can (15 ounces)	**kidney or black beans,** rinsed and **drained**
1 can (15 ounces)	**whole kernel corn,** drained
1 envelope	**taco seasoning**
1/2 cup	**water**
	sour cream
	grated cheddar cheese

In a 3- to 4-quart pot, brown beef and onion together until crumbly and done. Drain if necessary. Stir in remaining ingredients except sour cream and cheese. Simmer over low heat 15–25 minutes. Serve over crushed tortilla chips. Garnish with sour cream and grated cheddar cheese. Makes 6–8 servings.

CHEESY MEATBALL SOUP

2 1/2 cups	**water**
2	**beef bouillon cubes**
1 can (15 ounces)	**whole kernel corn,** with liquid
1	**medium potato,** peeled and cubed
1/2 cup	**sliced carrots**
1/2 cup	**chopped onion**
40	**frozen fully-cooked meatballs,** thawed*
1 jar (16 ounces)	**processed cheese sauce**

In a 4-quart pot, combine water, bouillon, corn, potato, carrots, and onion. Bring to a boil. Add meatballs. Bring to a boil again. Reduce heat. Cover and simmer for 20 minutes, or until potatoes are tender. Stir in the cheese sauce. Cook over low heat until heated through. Makes 4–6 servings.

*Can be found in the frozen meat section.

GRANDMA'S WINTER SOUP

1 pound **ground beef**
1 **large onion,** chopped
1 can (14.5 ounces) **diced tomatoes,** with liquid
1 package (16 ounces) **frozen mixed vegetables**
2 to 3 **beef bouillon cubes**
2 teaspoons **dried oregano**
4 cups **water**

In a saucepan, brown ground beef with onion until meat is no longer pink. Drain if necessary. Add remaining ingredients, and simmer over low heat 45 minutes to 1 hour. Makes 4 servings.

Sandwiches

BAKED HERO SANDWICHES

1 pound	**ground beef**
1	**medium onion,** halved and thinly sliced
1	**green bell pepper,** seeded and thinly sliced
2 tubes (10 to 13.8 ounces each)	**refrigerated pizza crust**
3 tablespoons	**honey mustard**
20 to 28	**slices Canadian bacon**
6 ounces	**sliced mozzarella or Monterey Jack cheese**
1 tablespoon	**butter or margarine,** melted

Preheat oven to 400 degrees.

In a frying pan, brown ground beef, onion, and bell pepper together until meat is no longer pink and vegetables are tender.

Spread one pizza crust over bottom of a greased 9 x 13-inch pan. Do not go up the sides. Spread honey mustard over the dough. Top evenly with hamburger mixture, Canadian bacon, and cheese. Unroll remaining tube of pizza dough over top. Stretch the dough to the edges. Bake 23–25 minutes, or until golden brown. Lightly brush butter over top. Allow sandwiches to cool for 10 minutes. Cut into 6–8 sandwiches to serve.

BARBEQUED BEEF

2 pounds	**ground beef**
1 envelope	**dry onion soup mix**
1/2 teaspoon	**salt**
1/2 teaspoon	**pepper**
1 1/2 cups	**ketchup**
2 tablespoons	**brown sugar**
10 to 12	**hamburger buns**

In a frying pan, brown ground beef until no longer pink. Drain if necessary. Stir in all remaining ingredients. Simmer over low heat for 20–30 minutes. Serve hot on hamburger buns. Makes 6–8 servings.

CHILI BEEF BARBEQUE

1 pound **ground beef**
1 **medium onion**
1 **green bell pepper,** seeded and chopped
1 can (7.75 ounces) **chili sauce**
2/3 cup **ketchup**
6 to 8 **whole wheat hamburger buns**

In a frying pan, brown ground beef with vegetables until meat is no longer pink. Stir in chili sauce and ketchup. Cover and simmer over low heat for 15–20 minutes, stirring occasionally. Serve hot on buns. Makes 6–8 servings.

GIANT MEATBALL SUB

25 **frozen fully-cooked meatballs***
1 jar (26 ounces) **spaghetti sauce,** any variety
1 teaspoon **minced garlic**
1 **loaf French bread**
mozzarella cheese, sliced

Heat meatballs according to package directions.

In a large frying pan, combine meatballs, spaghetti sauce, and garlic.

Cut bread in half lengthwise. Place bread halves cut side up on a baking sheet. Broil for 2 minutes until lightly toasted. Lay cheese slices over one of the halves. Spoon meatballs and sauce over cheese. Place the other bread half on top, cut side down. Cut into 6–8 single serve portions.

*Can be found in the frozen meat section.

GUMBO BURGERS

1 pound	**ground beef**
1	**medium onion,** chopped
1 can (10.75 ounces)	**chicken gumbo soup,** condensed
1/4 cup	**ketchup**
2 tablespoons	**mustard**
6 to 8	**hamburger buns**

In a frying pan, brown ground beef and onion together until meat is no longer pink. Drain if necessary. Add soup, ketchup, and mustard to cooked beef. Simmer over medium-low heat for 20 minutes, stirring occasionally. Serve on hamburger buns. Makes 6–8 servings.

OPEN-FACED STROGANOFF SUB

1 pound **ground beef**
1 **medium onion,** chopped
1 cup **sour cream**
1 tablespoon **Worcestershire sauce**
1 teaspoon **minced garlic**
1 loaf **French bread**
1 cup **grated Colby Jack cheese**

In a frying pan, brown ground beef and onion until meat is no longer pink. Drain if necessary. Stir in sour cream, Worcestershire sauce, and garlic. Warm over low heat.

Cut bread in half lengthwise. Broil bread cut side up 2 minutes until toasted. Spread hot meat over the top of bread halves. Sprinkle cheese over meat. Broil an additional 2 minutes, or until cheese melts. Makes 6–8 servings.

ENGLISH MUFFIN PIZZAS

1 pound **ground beef**
1 teaspoon **minced garlic**
1/2 teaspoon **Italian seasoning**
1 jar (14 ounces) **pizza sauce**
10 **English muffins,** split
2 cups **grated mozzarella cheese**

In a frying pan, brown ground beef and garlic until meat is no longer pink. Drain if necessary.

In a bowl, stir Italian seasoning into pizza sauce.

Broil English muffin halves on a baking sheet for 2–3 minutes, or until lightly toasted. Spread 1 tablespoon pizza sauce over each English muffin half. Spoon meat mixture evenly over top. Place halves back on baking sheet. Sprinkle cheese over each individual half. Broil for 2 minutes, or until cheese melts. Makes 7–10 servings.

TACO SANDWICHES

1 pound **ground beef**
$^{1}/_{2}$ cup **chopped onion**
1 can (8 ounces) **tomato sauce**
1 can (4 ounces) **chopped green chiles,** drained
$^{1}/_{2}$ envelope **taco seasoning**
6 to 8 **hamburger buns**
shredded lettuce
grated cheese
chopped tomatoes

In a frying pan, brown ground beef and onion until meat is no longer pink. Drain if necessary. Stir in tomato sauce, chiles, and taco seasoning. Simmer over low heat for 5 minutes. Serve on warmed buns and garnish with lettuce, cheese, and tomatoes. Makes 6–8 servings.

GRANDMA'S SLOPPY JOES

2 pounds **ground beef**
1 tablespoon **dried minced onion**
1 tablespoon **sugar**
2 tablespoons **mustard**
1 tablespoon **vinegar**
1 teaspoon **salt**
1 cup **ketchup**
8 to 10 **large hamburger buns**

In a frying pan, brown ground beef until meat is no longer pink. Drain if necessary. Stir in all remaining ingredients except hamburger buns. Cover and simmer over low heat for 25–30 minutes, stirring occasionally. Serve on warmed buns. Makes 8–10 servings.

GRILLED SWISS SANDWICHES

1/2 pound **ground beef**
1/4 cup **chopped onion**
1/3 cup **Thousand Island dressing**
6 **slices whole wheat or rye bread**
6 tablespoons **drained sauerkraut**
3 **slices Swiss cheese**
butter or margarine

In a frying pan, brown ground beef and onion until meat is no longer pink. Drain if necessary. Stir in dressing. Spoon meat mixture evenly over half the bread slices. Top each with 2 tablespoons sauerkraut, a slice of cheese, and remaining slices of bread. Grill sandwiches using a small amount of butter until lightly toasted and cheese melts. Makes 3 servings.

TEXAN PITAS

1 pound **ground beef**
1 envelope **taco seasoning**
1/2 cup **water**
1 can (16 ounces) **refried beans**
1 can (10 ounces) **tomatoes and diced green chiles,** with liquid
1/8 teaspoon **ground cumin**
6 **pita breads,** halved
1 cup **grated cheddar cheese**
sliced jalapenos

Preheat oven to 350 degrees.

In a large frying pan, brown ground beef until no longer pink. Drain if necessary. Add taco seasoning, water, refried beans, tomatoes and green chiles, and cumin. Simmer over low heat 15–20 minutes, stirring occasionally. Spoon about 1/3 cup of the meat mixture into pita bread. Top with about 2 tablespoons cheese and a few jalapenos. Place filled pita halves in an ungreased 9 x 13-inch baking pan. Bake for 10 minutes. Makes 5–7 servings.

Burgers & Grilled Sensations

BASIC BURGER

1/3 cup	**water**
1 envelope	**dry onion soup mix**
2 pounds	**ground beef**
6 to 8	**hamburger buns**

Heat gas, charcoal or electric grill.

In a 2-quart bowl, whisk water and dry onion soup mix together. Stir ground beef into soup mixture until thoroughly blended. Shape into 8 patties. Place patties on a hot grill. Grill for 12–16 minutes, turning once, until internal temperature reaches 165 degrees. Serve on buns with your favorite hamburger toppings. Makes 6–8 servings.

BARBEQUE MEATBALL KABOBS

1 **medium red onion,** cut into 12 wedges
12 **frozen fully-cooked meatballs,** thawed*
1 **medium zucchini,** cut into 12 1/2-inch-thick slices
12 **fresh mushrooms**
1 **yellow or orange bell pepper,** cut into 12 pieces
1/3 cup **honey barbeque sauce**

Heat gas, charcoal or electric grill.

Microwave onion wedges on high for 40 seconds to partially soften. Alternately place onion, meatballs, zucchini, mushrooms, and bell pepper onto six 12-inch metal skewers. Place kabobs on well-heated grill. Cover and grill for 15 minutes, turning kabobs every 2–3 minutes. During the last 3–5 minutes, brush barbeque sauce over the top to cover all sides. Cook until meatballs are heated and vegetables are done. Serve with additional barbeque sauce on the side. Makes 6 servings.

*Can be found in the frozen meat section.

GREEN CHILE BURGER

1 pound **ground beef**
1/3 cup **barbeque sauce**
1 can (4 ounces) **chopped green chiles, drained**
4 **slices Pepper Jack cheese**
4 **hamburger buns**
guacamole

Heat gas, charcoal or electric grill.

In a bowl, combine ground beef, barbeque sauce, and chiles. Shape into 4 patties. Grill patties for 12–16 minutes on a hot grill, turning once, until internal temperature reaches 165 degrees. Top with cheese and allow cheese to melt. Serve on buns with guacamole and your favorite hamburger toppings. Makes 4 servings.

COLBY SLOPPY JOE BURGER

1 1/2 pounds **ground beef**
1/4 cup **steak sauce**
1 envelope **sloppy joe seasoning mix**
6 **slices Colby Jack cheese**
6 **hamburger buns**

Heat gas, charcoal or electric grill.

In a bowl, combine ground beef, steak sauce, and sloppy joe seasoning. Form beef into 6 patties. Place patties on a hot grill. Cover and grill for 12–16 minutes, turning once. Cook until internal temperature reaches 165 degrees. Place cheese slices over patties during the last 1–2 minutes of cooking. Serve on buns with your favorite hamburger toppings. Makes 6 servings.

BARBEQUE MEAT LOAF PATTIES

1 1/2 pounds **ground beef**
3/4 cup **dry instant oatmeal**
1 cup **milk**
3 tablespoons **dried minced onion**
1 1/2 teaspoons **salt**
1/4 teaspoon **pepper**
1 bottle (18 ounces) **barbeque sauce**

Heat gas, charcoal or electric grill.

In a bowl, combine ground beef, oatmeal, milk, onion, salt, and pepper. Form 8 patties. Place patties on a hot grill. Cover and grill for 15–17 minutes, turning once half way through. Brush barbeque sauce over top during last few minutes of cooking. Cook until internal temperature reaches 165 degrees. Serve with mashed potatoes and a green salad. Makes 8 servings.

EASY TIN FOIL DINNERS

6 to 8 **medium red potatoes,** cut into bite-sized pieces
1 **medium red onion,** cut into 12 wedges
2 teaspoons **Italian seasoning**
1 teaspoon **salt**
1 tablespoon **olive oil**
4 (1/4 pound each) **frozen lean ground beef patties**

Heat gas, charcoal or electric grill.

Cut four 18 x 12-inch sheets of aluminum foil. Spray shiny side with nonstick cooking spray. In a microwave-safe bowl, toss potatoes, onion, Italian seasoning, salt, and oil together. Microwave on high for 3–4 minutes to partially cook vegetables.

Place a beef patty in the center of each aluminum sheet. Divide potatoes and onion mixture evenly over the patties. Fold the aluminum foil in half over the meat and vegetable mixture. Fold the edges twice, leaving extra room for heat expansion. Place the dinners over the hot grill. Cover and cook 20–25 minutes over medium heat, or until patties reach 165 degrees internally, and potatoes are tender. Makes 4 servings.

FRENCH ONION BURGER

1 pound	**ground beef**
2/3 cup	**French onion sour cream dip,** divided
3 tablespoons	**seasoned breadcrumbs**
1/4 teaspoon	**salt**
4	**hamburger buns**

Heat gas, charcoal or electric grill.

Combine ground beef, 1/3 cup French onion dip, breadcrumbs, and salt. Shape meat mixture into 4 equally-sized patties. Grill over a hot grill for 15 minutes, turning once until internal temperature reaches 165 degrees. Spread remaining French onion dip on bottom of hamburger buns. Serve on buns with your favorite hamburger toppings. Makes 4 servings.

VARIATION: Top burgers with a slice of Swiss cheese.

GUACAMOLE BURGER

1 1/2 pounds	**ground beef**
1	**egg,** beaten
1 teaspoon	**salt**
1/4 teaspoon	**pepper**
1 container (12 ounces)	**guacamole**
4	**hamburger buns**

Heat gas, charcoal or electric grill.

In a bowl, combine ground beef, egg, salt, and pepper. Shape meat mixture into 8 thin patties. Spoon a heaping tablespoon of guacamole on center of 4 patties. Top with remaining patties, and seal edges. Grill or fry hamburgers until meat temperature reaches 165 degrees and is no longer pink. Serve on buns with extra guacamole and favorite hamburger toppings. Makes 4 servings.

JACK O'LANTERN BURGERS

1 pound **ground beef**
1 teaspoon **salt**
4 **slices American cheese**
4 **hamburger buns**

Heat gas, charcoal or electric grill.

In a bowl, combine ground beef and salt. Shape into 4 hamburger patties. Grill or fry hamburgers until meat temperature reaches 165 degrees and meat is no longer pink. Cut eyes, nose, and mouth out of each slice of American cheese. Place cheese on burger and heat until melted (about 1 minute). Serve open-faced on buns with your favorite toppings on the side. Makes 4 servings.

STUFFED ONION BURGERS

1 1/2 cups **chopped onion**
2 tablespoons **butter or margarine**
2 tablespoons **mustard**
1 1/2 teaspoons **salt,** divided
1 1/2 pounds **ground beef**
1/2 teaspoon **pepper**
6 **hamburger buns**

Heat gas, charcoal or electric grill.

In a frying pan, saute onions in butter until tender. Stir in mustard and 1/2 teaspoon salt.

In a separate bowl, combine ground beef, remaining salt, and pepper. Shape meat mixture into 12 thin patties. Spread onion mixture over 6 patties. Top with remaining patties and seal around edges. Grill, turning once until meat reaches 165 degrees and is no longer pink in the center. Serve on buns with your favorite toppings. Makes 6 servings.

SWISS MUSHROOM BURGERS

6 **frozen hamburger patties**
1 package (6 ounces) **sliced fresh mushrooms**
2 tablespoons **olive oil**
6 **slices Swiss cheese**
6 **hamburger buns**

Heat gas, charcoal or electric grill.

Grill hamburger patties for 7 minutes on each side, or until done.

While hamburgers are grilling, saute mushrooms in oil over medium heat. Lay a slice of cheese over each burger during the last minute of grilling. Lay each burger over bottom of bun. Spoon mushrooms over cheese. Top with the top of bun. Serve immediately. Makes 6 servings.

BACON-WRAP BURGER

1/2 cup	**grated cheddar cheese**
1 tablespoon	**grated Parmesan cheese**
1/2 cup	**chopped onion**
1	**egg**
1 tablespoon	**Worcestershire sauce**
1/2 teaspoon	**salt**
1/4 teaspoon	**pepper**
1 pound	**ground beef**
6	**slices bacon**
6	**hamburger buns**

Heat gas, charcoal or electric grill.

In a 2-quart bowl, combine cheeses, onion, egg, Worcestershire sauce, salt, and pepper. Stir in ground beef until thoroughly combined. Shape meat mixture into 6 patties. Wrap a slice of bacon around each patty. Secure bacon with toothpicks. Place patties on a hot grill. Grill for 7–8 minutes on both sides, or until meat reaches 165 degrees and is no longer pink in the center. Remove toothpicks and serve on hamburger buns with your favorite hamburger toppings. Makes 6 servings.

Meat Loaf

AVOCADO MEAT LOAF

2 pounds	**ground beef**
3/4 cup	**diced celery**
1/2 cup	**chopped green onion**
1 tablespoon	**parsley**
1/2 cup	**diced green bell pepper**
1 can (8 ounces)	**tomato sauce**
1 cup	**dry breadcrumbs**
1 1/2 to 2 cups	**chopped fresh mushrooms**
1	**egg,** beaten
1	**large avocado,** skinned and diced
1 teaspoon	**celery salt**
1/2 teaspoon	**pepper**
1 tablespoon	**paprika**

Preheat oven to 350 degrees.

In a large bowl, combine all ingredients except paprika, and mix well. Press meat mixture into a greased loaf pan. Sprinkle paprika over meat loaf. Bake 90 minutes, or until no longer pink in the middle. Makes 6–8 servings.

LISA'S MEAT LOAF

1 pound **ground beef**
1 cup **dry breadcrumbs**
3/4 cup **mashed bananas**
1/2 **small onion,** finely chopped
1/2 teaspoon **paprika**
1/2 teaspoon **dry mustard**
2 teaspoons **salt**
1/2 teaspoon **pepper**

Preheat oven to 350 degrees.

In a bowl, combine all ingredients and mix well. Shape into loaf and place in a greased loaf pan. Bake for 1 hour, or until no longer pink in the middle. Makes 4 servings.

BLUE CHEESE MEAT LOAF

2 pounds **ground beef**
1 container (4 ounces) **crumbled blue cheese**
1/2 cup **Italian seasoned breadcrumbs**
1/2 cup **dried minced onion**
2 tablespoons **oregano or parsley**
1/4 cup **milk**
1 teaspoon **salt**

Preheat oven to 350 degrees.

In a large bowl, combine all ingredients. Press meat mixture into a greased loaf pan. Bake 60 minutes, or until internal temperature reaches 165 degrees. Makes 6–8 servings.

INDIVIDUAL MEAT LOAVES

2 **eggs,** beaten
1 can (10.5 ounces) **onion soup,** condensed
1 1/2 cups **breadcrumbs**
2 tablespoons **Italian seasoning**
1 teaspoon **Worcestershire sauce**
1/2 teaspoon **salt**
2 pounds **ground beef**
ketchup

Preheat oven to 350 degrees.

In a large bowl, combine eggs, soup, breadcrumbs, seasoning, Worcestershire sauce, and salt. Mix beef into egg mixture until well blended. Divide meat into 12 balls. Press into muffin pans. Bake for 25–30 minutes. Spread desired amount of ketchup over individual loaves for last 5–10 minutes of cooking. Makes 8–12 servings.

MAC 'N' CHEESE MEAT LOAF

1 pound **ground beef**
1/2 cup **dry macaroni noodles,** cooked according to package directions
1/2 cup **dry breadcrumbs**
1/2 cup **milk**
2 **eggs,** beaten
1/2 **small onion,** chopped
1/4 cup **chopped green bell pepper**
1/3 cup **grated cheddar cheese**
1 teaspoon **salt**
1/4 teaspoon **pepper**

Preheat oven to 350 degrees.

In a large bowl, combine all ingredients and mix well. Shape into a loaf and place in a greased loaf pan. Bake for 1 hour, or until no longer pink in the middle. Makes 4–6 servings.

POLYNESIAN MEAT LOAF

1 pound **ground beef**
1 pound **ground pork**
1 1/2 cups **dry breadcrumbs**
2 **eggs,** beaten
1/2 cup **pineapple juice**
1/2 teaspoon **marjoram**
1 teaspoon **dry mustard**
2 teaspoons **salt**
1/2 teaspoon **pepper**
2/3 cup **crushed pineapple**

Preheat oven to 350 degrees.

In a large bowl, combine all ingredients except crushed pineapple. Shape into a loaf and place in a greased loaf pan. Bake for 50 minutes. Remove from oven and place pineapple chunks on top. Return to oven and bake an additional 20 minutes, or until no longer pink in the middle. Makes 6–8 servings.

POTATO-COVERED MEAT LOAF

1 pound **ground beef**
1 can (8 ounces) **tomato sauce**
1/2 cup **milk**
1 **small onion,** chopped
1/2 cup **dry breadcrumbs**
1 tablespoon **ketchup**
1/2 teaspoon **dry mustard**
1 **egg,** beaten
1/4 cup **chopped green bell pepper**
2 teaspoons **Worcestershire sauce**
1 teaspoon **salt**
1/4 teaspoon **pepper**
1/4 cup **chopped green onions**
2 cups **prepared mashed potatoes***

Preheat oven to 350 degrees.

In a large bowl, combine all ingredients except green onion and mashed potatoes. Shape into a loaf and place in a greased loaf pan. Bake for 40 minutes. Remove from oven.

In a small bowl, combine green onion and mashed potatoes. Spread mixture over top of meat loaf and return to oven for an additional 30 minutes. Makes 4–6 servings.

*Instant mashed potatoes work well here.

PINEAPPLE MEAT LOAF

1 pound **ground beef**
1 can (8 ounces) **crushed pineapple,** with liquid
1/2 cup **seasoned breadcrumbs**
2 **eggs,** slightly beaten
1 teaspoon **salt**
1 teaspoon **Worcestershire sauce**
2 tablespoons **ketchup**
1/4 cup **pineapple juice**

Preheat oven to 350 degrees.

In a large bowl, combine beef, pineapple, breadcrumbs, eggs, salt, and Worcestershire sauce. Form into a loaf and place in a greased loaf pan. Bake for 55 minutes and then remove from oven.

In a bowl, combine ketchup and juice. Pour sauce over top of meat loaf. Bake an additional 5–10 minutes, or until internal temperature reaches 165 degrees. Makes 4–6 servings.

MEAT LOAF IN AN ONION

1 pound **ground beef**
1 **egg,** slightly beaten
1/4 cup **dry breadcrumbs**
1/4 cup **tomato sauce**
1/8 teaspoon **pepper**
1/2 teaspoon **salt**
1/2 teaspoon **dry mustard**
6 **large onions,** peeled

Preheat oven to 350 degrees.

In a medium bowl, combine ground beef, egg, breadcrumbs, tomato sauce, pepper, salt, and mustard. Set aside.

Cut onions in half horizontally and remove centers, leaving 1/4-inch-thick shell. Chop onion centers and add 3 tablespoons to meat mixture. Spoon mixture into 6 onion halves. Top with remaining onion halves. Roll in aluminum foil. Bake 25–35 minutes, or until meat is no longer pink. Makes 6 servings.

SOUTHWESTERN MEAT LOAF

1 pound **ground beef**
1 cup **frozen whole kernel corn**
3/4 cup **salsa**
1/3 cup **uncooked regular oatmeal**
2 tablespoons **dried chopped cilantro**
1/2 cup **chopped onion**
1 tablespoon **chili powder**
1 **egg,** slightly beaten
3 tablespoons **ketchup**

Preheat oven to 375 degrees.

Combine all ingredients except ketchup. Press meat mixture into a loaf pan. Spread ketchup over top. Bake for 50 minutes, or until internal temperature reaches 165 degrees, or until meat is no longer pink in the middle. Makes 4–6 servings.

STUFFED APPLE MEAT LOAF

2 pounds **ground beef**
1 box (6 ounces) **stuffing mix**
2 cups **finely chopped apples**
3 **eggs,** slightly beaten
1 1/2 teaspoons **salt**
2 tablespoons **mustard**
1 **medium onion,** chopped
1 cup **ketchup**

Preheat oven to 350 degrees.

Mix together all ingredients. Place the meat mixture evenly in 2 loaf pans. Bake 60–65 minutes, until meat is no longer pink, or until internal temperature reaches 165 degrees. Makes 8–10 servings.

*One pan can be frozen and baked at a later date. If frozen, thaw loaf in the refrigerator 24 hours before baking.

BABY MEAT LOAVES

1 1/2 pounds **ground beef**
1 cup **dry fine breadcrumbs**
1/2 cup **chopped walnuts**
1/4 cup **chili sauce**
1 1/2 teaspoons **seasoning salt**
1/2 cup **milk**

Preheat oven to 350 degrees.

In a bowl, combine all ingredients and shape into 4 small loaves. Place each loaf in greased mini loaf pans and bake 35 minutes, or until meat is no longer pink. Makes 4 servings.

YUMMY MEAT ROLL

1 1/2 pounds **ground beef**
3/4 cup **saltine cracker crumbs**
1 **egg,** slightly beaten
1/2 cup **chopped onion**
1 teaspoon **Italian seasoning**
1 teaspoon **salt**
1/2 teaspoon **pepper**
2 cans (8 ounces each) **tomato sauce, divided**
2 cups **grated mozzarella cheese**
1/3 cup **grated Parmesan cheese**

Preheat oven to 350 degrees.

In a large bowl, combine the first seven ingredients with 1/3 cup tomato sauce. On wax paper, press the meat mixture into a 10 x 12-inch rectangle. Sprinkle mozzarella cheese over top. Roll jelly-roll style starting with longer end. Press ends to seal. Bake in a 10 x 15 x 1-inch pan for 1 hour. Drain any excess fat. Pour remaining tomato sauce over top. Sprinkle Parmesan cheese over top and bake an additional 10–15 minutes, or until done. Makes 6 servings.

Main Dishes

BEEFED-UP SPAGHETTI

1 pound	**ground beef**
1 jar (26 ounces)	**chunky spaghetti sauce**
1 can (8 ounces)	**tomato sauce**
1 teaspoon	**minced garlic**
1 teaspoon	**Italian seasoning**
1 package (16 ounces)	**spaghetti noodles,** cooked

In a frying pan, brown ground beef until no longer pink. Drain if necessary. Stir in spaghetti sauce, tomato sauce, garlic, and seasoning. Simmer over low heat 5–10 minutes while noodles are cooking. Serve over hot cooked spaghetti. Makes 6 servings.

VARIATION: 1 can (4 ounces) sliced mushrooms, drained, may also be added.

BARBEQUE PIZZA

1 pound **ground beef**
3/4 cup **barbeque sauce**
1 **small red onion,** chopped
1 **pre-made pizza crust**
1 1/2 cups **grated Colby Jack cheese**

Preheat oven to 400 degrees.

In a frying pan, brown ground beef until no longer pink. Drain if necessary. Stir barbeque sauce and onion into beef. Simmer over low heat for 5 minutes.

Place crust on a pizza pan. Spoon beef mixture over top. Sprinkle cheese over meat mixture. Bake for 10 minutes, or until done. Makes 4 servings.

CORN-CRUSTED BEEF DISH

2 pounds **ground beef**
3 **medium onions,** chopped
1 1/2 teaspoons **ground cumin**
1 can (4 ounces) **sliced mushrooms,** drained
4 cans (15 ounces each) **whole kernel corn,** drained
1 1/2 teaspoons **basil**
1 teaspoon **salt**
1/2 teaspoon **pepper**
3 tablespoons **butter or margarine**
1 tablespoon **cornstarch**
2 tablespoons **sugar**

Preheat oven to 400 degrees.

In a frying pan, brown beef and onions until meat is no longer pink. Drain if necessary. Stir cumin into beef mixture. Spoon beef mixture into bottom of a greased 9 x 13-inch pan. Sprinkle mushrooms evenly over meat.

In a blender, grind corn for 3 minutes. Pour liquefied corn into a saucepan with basil, salt, pepper, and butter. Heat until it starts to bubble. Slowly stir in cornstarch to thicken. Sprinkle corn mixture evenly over beef. Sprinkle sugar over top. Bake 40–50 minutes, or until golden brown. Makes 6–8 servings.

CAMPER'S POTLUCK DINNER

1 pound **ground beef**
1 teaspoon **salt**
1 can (16 ounces) **small white potatoes,** drained
1 can (16 ounces) **mixed vegetables,** with liquid
1 can (16 ounces) **small whole onions,** drained
2 jars (11 ounces each) **beef gravy**

In a medium bowl, combine ground beef and salt. Shape ground beef into 6 patties. Brown the patties in a large frying pan about 8 minutes, or until meat is no longer pink.

In a bowl, combine potatoes, vegetables, onions, and gravy. Pour over cooked meat patties. Heat through about 5 minutes. Serve each patty with a spoonful of vegetable mixture. Makes 6 servings.

BEEF AND POTATO PIE

1 1/2 pounds **ground beef**
2 **large potatoes,** peeled and cubed
salt and pepper
1 container (16 ounces) **cottage cheese**
2 **eggs**
1/2 cup **sour cream**
1 teaspoon **oregano**
2 **deep-dish pie shells**
2 cups **grated cheddar cheese**

In a frying pan, brown ground beef until no longer pink. Drain if necessary.

In a pot, boil potatoes in salted water until tender. Drain and mash potatoes. Season with salt and pepper to taste.

In a blender, blend cottage cheese, eggs, sour cream, and oregano until smooth. Stir cottage cheese mixture into potatoes. Divide ground beef between the two pie shells. Spread potato mixture evenly over ground beef. Sprinkle cheese over top. Bake for 30–35 minutes and serve. Makes 8–12 servings.

GINGER BEEF BOK CHOY

1 1/2 pounds **ground beef**
1 **large onion,** sliced
1 **head bok choy,** cut into bite-sized pieces
1 teaspoon **ginger**
1 teaspoon **minced garlic**
1/2 cup **soy sauce**
1/3 cup **sugar**
1 cup **beef broth**
1 block (14 ounces) **tofu,** drained and cubed

In a large wok or 3- to 4-quart pan, brown ground beef until no longer pink and then remove with a slotted spoon and set aside. Cook onion for 2–3 minutes. Add bok choy, and cook until tender. Stir in cooked beef, ginger, garlic, soy sauce, sugar, and broth. Simmer over low heat for 5 minutes. Add tofu to pan. Simmer until tofu is heated through. Makes 8–10 servings.

EASY ITALIAN PASTA SKILLET

1 pound **ground beef**
1/2 **large onion,** chopped
1/2 cup **finely chopped celery**
2 cans (14.5 ounces each) **Italian-style diced tomatoes,** with liquid
1 can (2.25 ounces) **sliced olives,** drained
2 cups **dry elbow macaroni**
1/4 cup **water**
1 cup **grated mozzarella cheese**

In a frying pan, brown ground beef and onion until meat is no longer pink. Add all remaining ingredients except cheese. Bring to a boil. Reduce heat and cover. Simmer over low heat for 20–25, minutes stirring occasionally. Cook until pasta is done. Sprinkle cheese over top and let melt. Makes 4–6 servings.

BARNEY'S SLOW-COOKED BEANS

1 pound **ground beef**
1 **medium onion,** chopped
1 pound **bacon,** cooked and crumbled
1 can (31 ounces) **pork and beans**
1 can (15 ounces) **garbanzo beans,** drained
1 can (16 ounces) **kidney beans,** drained
1 can (15.25 ounces) **black beans,** drained and rinsed
1 cup **ketchup**
1/2 cup **brown sugar**
1 can (8 ounces) **tomato sauce**
1 tablespoon **seasoning salt**
1 tablespoon **garlic pepper**
1 tablespoon **hot sauce** (optional)

In a frying pan, brown ground beef and onion until meat is no longer pink. Drain if necessary. Combine beef mixture and remaining ingredients in a greased 5- to 7-quart slow cooker. Cover and cook on low heat for 4–5 hours. Makes 10–12 servings.

LASAGNA ROLL-UPS

1/2 pound **ground beef**
1 **small onion,** chopped
1 teaspoon **garlic salt**
1 jar (28 ounces) **chunky spaghetti sauce,** divided
2 cups **Italian-blend grated cheese,** divided
8 **lasagna noodles,** cooked and drained*

Preheat oven to 375 degrees.

In a large frying pan, brown ground beef and onion until meat is no longer pink. Drain if necessary. Remove from heat. Sprinkle with garlic salt. Add 1/2 cup spaghetti sauce. Allow meat to cool and then add 1 cup cheese. Spread 1 cup spaghetti sauce into bottom of a 9 x 9-inch pan. Spoon 1/2 cup meat mixture down center of each lasagna noodle; roll up and place seam side down in pan. Spread remaining sauce over roll-ups.

Cover pan with aluminum foil. Bake for 35 minutes or until heated through. Sprinkle with remaining cheese. Bake an additional 5 minutes, or until cheese melts. Let stand 5 minutes before serving. Makes 6 servings.

*You may want to cook 10 noodles in case any break.

CUBAN BEEF AND POTATOES OVER RICE

1 pound **ground beef**
2 cans (15 ounces each) **tomato sauce**
1/3 cup **chopped onion**
1/2 cup **chopped green bell pepper**
1 tablespoon **capers**
1 1/2 teaspoons **onion powder**
1 teaspoon **garlic powder**
1 **bay leaf**
3 to 5 **large potatoes,** peeled and cubed
3 cups **hot cooked rice**
3 **bananas,** sliced (optional)

In a large frying pan, brown ground beef until no longer pink. Drain if necessary.

In a bowl, combine tomato sauce, onion, bell pepper, capers, onion powder, garlic powder, and bay leaf. Pour into ground beef. Stir in potatoes, bring to a boil, and then reduce heat. Cover and simmer over low heat 45 minutes to 1 hour, stirring often, or until potatoes are fork tender. Remove bay leaf and serve meat mixture over hot cooked rice. For an authentic Cuban taste, garnish with sliced bananas. Makes 4–6 servings.

STUFFED TACO PASTA SHELLS

1 pound	**ground beef**
1 envelope	**taco seasoning mix**
1 3/4 cups	**salsa,** divided
1 package (12 ounces)	**jumbo pasta shells,** cooked and drained
1 1/2 cups	**grated Mexican-blend cheese**

Preheat oven to 350 degrees.

In a large frying pan, brown ground beef until no longer pink. Drain if necessary. Stir in the taco seasoning and 3/4 cup salsa; simmer for 2 minutes. Remove from heat. Fill cooked jumbo pasta shells with 1 tablespoon meat mixture. Lay stuffed shells in bottom of a greased 9 x 13-inch baking dish. Spoon remaining salsa over shells; top with cheese. Cover pan with aluminum foil. Bake for 30 minutes, or until hot and cheese has melted. Makes 6–8 servings.

ASPARAGUS SHEPHERD'S PIE

1 pound	**ground beef**
1	**medium onion,** chopped
1 teaspoon	**minced garlic**
1 can (15 ounces)	**asparagus,** drained
2 cups	**prepared mashed potatoes***

Preheat oven to 350 degrees.

In a frying pan, brown ground beef, onion, and garlic until meat is no longer pink. Drain if necessary. Spread meat mixture into bottom of a greased 8 x 8- or 9 x 9-inch pan. Lay asparagus evenly over meat mixture. Spread mashed potatoes evenly over asparagus. Bake uncovered for 15–20 minutes, or until thoroughly heated. Makes 4–6 servings.

*Instant mashed potatoes work well here.

MEATBALL STROGANOFF

1 pound **ground beef**
1/2 **medium onion,** chopped
1 **egg**
1/4 cup **seasoned breadcrumbs**
1/2 teaspoon **salt**
1/2 teaspoon **pepper**
1 can (10.5 ounces) **cream of mushroom soup,** condensed
1/2 cup **sour cream**
1/3 cup **water**
3 cups **cooked egg noodles**

In a bowl, combine ground beef, onion, egg, breadcrumbs, salt, and pepper. Form into 16 meatballs. Brown in a frying pan. Drain if necessary. Stir in soup, sour cream, and water. Cover and simmer over low heat for 10 minutes. Serve over hot egg noodles. Makes 4 servings.

JACKPOT CASSEROLE

1 pound **ground beef**
1 tablespoon **sugar**
1/2 teaspoon **garlic salt**
2 cans (8 ounces each) **tomato sauce**
2 tablespoons **water**
1 package (4 ounces) **cream cheese,** softened
1/2 cup **milk**
1 cup **light sour cream**
1 package (8 ounces) **elbow macaroni,** cooked according to package directions
2 cups **grated cheddar cheese**

Preheat oven to 350 degrees.

In a large frying pan, brown ground beef until no longer pink. Drain if necessary. Add sugar, garlic salt, tomato sauce, and water to ground beef. Simmer for 5 minutes.

In a small bowl, combine cream cheese, milk, and sour cream.

In a greased 9 x 13-inch pan, layer half the cooked noodles, half the sauce and 1 cup cheese. Repeat layers. Bake 30 minutes. Makes 6–8 servings.

OKRA AND BEEF SKILLET

2 pounds **ground beef**
2 cans (8 ounces each) **tomato sauce**
1 tablespoon **southwestern seasoning or chili powder**
1 can (15.25 ounces) **whole kernel corn,** with liquid
1 package (16 ounces) **frozen okra,** thawed and cut into bite-sized pieces
1 cup **grated Mexican-blend cheese**

In a large frying pan, brown ground beef until no longer pink. Drain if necessary. Stir in tomato sauce, seasoning, corn, and okra. Bring to a boil. Cover and reduce heat. Simmer for 10 minutes, stirring occasionally. Sprinkle cheese over top and serve. Makes 8–10 servings.

STUFFED EGGPLANT

2 **medium eggplants,** halved
1 pound **ground beef**
1 can (16 ounces) **stewed tomatoes,** with liquid
1 can (8 ounces) **tomato sauce**
1 teaspoon **salt**
1/4 teaspoon **oregano**
1/4 teaspoon **garlic salt**
1/2 cup **grated Parmesan cheese**

Preheat oven to 350 degrees.

Cut ends from eggplants. Carefully cut each eggplant lengthwise down the center, and scoop out flesh, leaving a 1/4-inch shell and making sure not to break. Place eggplant shells in a baking pan and set aside. Chop eggplant centers and add to a large frying pan with ground beef. Brown ground beef until no longer pink. Add tomatoes, tomato sauce, salt, oregano, and garlic salt. Simmer over low heat 15–20 minutes, stirring occasionally. Remove from heat and stir in Parmesan cheese. Spoon meat mixture into the eggplant shells. Bake 25 minutes, or until eggplant shell is tender. Makes 4 servings.

SALSA-RICE-HAMBURGER SKILLET

1 pound	**ground beef**
1 can (14.5 ounces)	**stewed tomatoes,** with liquid
1 can (15.25 ounces)	**black beans,** rinsed and drained
1 cup	**uncooked rice**
1 can (14.5 ounces)	**beef broth**
2/3 cup	**salsa**
1 teaspoon	**chili powder**

In a frying pan, brown ground beef until no longer pink. Drain if necessary. Add remaining ingredients to cooked beef. Bring to a boil. Reduce heat to low. Cover and simmer for 20–25 minutes, or until rice is done. Let stand 5 minutes before serving. Makes 4–6 servings.

STUFFED TOMATOES

6 **medium tomatoes**
1 pound **ground beef**
1/4 cup **minced onion**
1 cup **milk**
1/4 cup **flour**
1 teaspoon **salt**
1/4 teaspoon **pepper**
1 teaspoon **curry powder**
1/2 cup **buttered breadcrumbs**

Preheat oven to 350 degrees.

Cut a very thin slice from the top of tomatoes and carefully spoon out centers. Turn tomato "cups" upside down to drain and set aside.

In a frying pan, brown ground beef with onion until meat is no longer pink and onion is transparent.

In a small bowl, combine milk, flour, salt, pepper, and curry. Pour mixture into meat and bring to a boil over medium-low heat and boil 1 minute. Spoon meat mixture into tomato cups. Place tomato cups in a baking pan and sprinkle tops with buttered breadcrumbs. Bake 17–20 minutes, or until golden brown. Makes 6 servings.

CABBAGE AND BEEF POTPIE

1 pound	**ground beef**
1	**medium onion,** chopped
1 bag (16 ounces)	**shredded cabbage and carrot coleslaw blend**
2 1/4 cups	**water,** divided
2 envelopes (.87 ounces each)	**brown gravy mix**
2	**frozen ready-to-bake piecrusts,** thawed

Preheat oven to 375 degrees.

In a large frying pan, brown ground beef and onion until no longer pink. Drain if necessary. Add coleslaw blend and 1 cup water. Cover and simmer over low heat, stirring occasionally, until vegetables are almost done. Stir in gravy mix and remaining water. Simmer until gravy thickens. Lay one crust in a deep-dish pie pan. Spoon beef mixture into pie shell. Cover with remaining crust; seal edges. Cut a few short slits in the top crust to allow steam to vent during baking. Bake 23–28 minutes, or until golden brown. Let stand for 5 minutes before serving. Makes 4–6 servings.

SWEDISH MEATBALLS

1 pound	**ground beef**
1	**egg,** slightly beaten
1/2 cup	**fine dry breadcrumbs**
1/3 cup	**milk**
2 tablespoons	**dry minced onion**
1 tablespoon	**brown sugar**
1/4 teaspoon	**ground nutmeg**
1/8 teaspoon	**allspice**
1/4 cup	**flour**
1 can (10.75 ounces)	**cream of chicken soup,** condensed
1 1/2 cups	**water**
1 package (12 ounces)	**egg noodles**

In a medium bowl, combine all ingredients except flour, soup, water, and noodles. Shape into 16 meatballs. Roll meatballs in flour and place in a large frying pan. Over medium heat, cook meatballs until lightly browned and no longer pink in the middle. Drain if necessary.

In a small bowl, whisk together soup and water until smooth, and add to frying pan. Heat to boiling over medium-high heat, reduce heat to low and simmer for 20 minutes. Serve over hot cooked noodles. Makes 4 servings.

TRACY'S HAMBURGER RICE

1 pound **ground beef**
1 **medium onion,** chopped
1 can (4 ounces) **sliced mushrooms,** drained
1 **red bell pepper,** seeded and chopped
3 cups **cooked rice***
soy sauce

In a large frying pan, brown ground beef until no longer pink. Stir onion, mushrooms, and bell pepper into beef. Saute until onions are transparent. Stir in cooked rice. Serve in bowls. Top individual servings with desired amount of soy sauce. Makes 4–6 servings.

*2 cups dry minute rice yields 3 cooked cups.

Family Favorites

EMPANADA PIE

1 pound **ground beef**
2 **onions,** chopped
2 teaspoons **paprika**
1 teaspoon **cumin**
1 teaspoon **salt**
1/3 cup **raisins**
1/2 cup **sliced black olives**
2 **refrigerated 9-inch pie crusts**

Preheat oven to 400 degrees.

In a pan, brown ground beef and onions until meat is no longer pink. Stir in paprika, cumin, and salt. Remove from heat. Stir in raisins and olives.

Lay one crust in a deep-dish pie pan. Spoon meat mixture into pie crust. Lay second crust over top and seal edges by pinching together. Cut four slits in top crust to allow steam to escape. Bake 30 minutes, or until golden. Makes 10 servings.

PACO'S TACO SALAD

1 pound	**ground beef**
1 bottle (16 ounces)	**Catalina salad dressing**
1 can (15 ounces)	**kidney beans,** drained
1 envelope	**taco seasoning**
1	**cucumber,** seeded and diced
1	**avocado,** peeled and chopped
1 can (2.25 ounces)	**diced olives**
1/2 cup	**diced green bell pepper**
1	**bunch green onions,** diced
1 head	**lettuce,** shredded
1 package (15.6 ounces)	**nacho cheese–flavored chips,** crushed

In a frying pan, brown ground beef until no longer pink. Drain if necessary. Add Catalina dressing, beans, and taco seasoning; heat through.

In a large bowl, combine other ingredients and toss well. Top with warm meat mixture, combine, and serve immediately. Makes 6 servings.

CHEESEBURGER PIZZA

1 tube (13.8 ounces)	**refrigerated pizza crust**
1/2 to 1 pound	**ground beef**
1	**medium onion,** diced
1 teaspoon	**barbeque seasoning**
1 teaspoon	**Italian seasoning**
1 can (8 ounces)	**tomato sauce**
2 cups	**grated cheddar cheese**

Preheat oven to 400 degrees.

Spread crust over greased baking sheet. Bake 8 minutes.

In a frying pan, brown ground beef and onion until meat is no longer pink. Stir in barbeque seasoning.

In a bowl, stir Italian seasoning into tomato sauce. Spread sauce over crust. Sprinkle seasoned meat and then cheese over sauce. Bake 9–11 minutes, or until cheese is melted and crust is lightly golden. Makes 6–8 servings.

CONEY DOGS

1 pound **ground beef**
1 **medium onion,** chopped
1 envelope **sloppy joe mix**
ingredients used for sloppy joe mix
1/2 teaspoon **chili powder**
1 package **hot dogs**
1 package **hot dog buns,** warmed
grated cheddar cheese

In a frying pan, brown ground beef and onion together until meat is no longer pink. Add sloppy joe seasonings, ingredients called for on mix, and chili powder. Simmer over low heat for 5–10 minutes.

Cook hot dogs according to package directions. Place hot dogs in buns, and top with beef sauce. Garnish with grated cheddar cheese if desired. Makes 8–10 servings.

DINNER PATTIES

1/2 pound **ground beef**
1 **small onion,** chopped
1/4 cup **chopped green bell pepper**
1 can (8 ounces) **cream-style corn**
1/2 teaspoon **salt**
1 cup **dry pancake mix**
1 **egg**
1 cup **milk**

Brown ground beef, onion, and bell pepper together. Drain if necessary. Stir in corn and salt and then set aside.

In a small bowl, combine pancake mix, egg, and milk. Fold into meat mixture.

On a heated frying pan, drop 1/4 cup at a time of the pancake mixture. Cook on each side for about 2 1/2 minutes, or until lightly browned. Serve with ketchup or favorite chili sauce. Makes 4–6 pancakes.

MEAT PIES

1 pound **ground beef**
1 **small onion,** minced
1 **egg,** slightly beaten
$^1/_2$ cup **dry fine breadcrumbs**
1 tablespoon **ketchup**
$^1/_2$ teaspoon **Worcestershire sauce**
1 teaspoon **salt**
$^1/_4$ teaspoon **pepper**
1 package (15 ounces) **refrigerated piecrusts**

Preheat oven to 400 degrees.

In a large frying pan, brown ground beef with onion until meat is no longer pink and onion is transparent. Drain if necessary.

In a bowl, combine egg, breadcrumbs, ketchup, Worcestershire sauce, salt, and pepper. Pour mixture into meat, heat through and set aside.

Open piecrusts and press each into a 12-inch square. Cut each square piecrust into four 6-inch squares. Spoon about $^1/_4$ cup meat mixture onto each square. Fold over crust to make a triangle. Press edges with a fork to seal. Bake 20 minutes or until piecrust is lightly browned. Makes 4 servings.

BAKED ITALIAN DELIGHT

1 pound	**ground beef**
1 jar (26 ounces)	**chunky spaghetti sauce**
1 cup	**cottage cheese**
1/4 cup	**grated Parmesan cheese**
1	**egg,** slightly beaten
2 tubes (8-count each)	**crescent rolls**
1 cup	**grated mozzarella cheese**

Preheat oven to 375 degrees.

In a large frying pan, brown ground beef until no longer pink. Drain if necessary. Stir spaghetti sauce into cooked beef. Simmer 5 minutes over low heat.

In a bowl, combine cottage cheese, Parmesan cheese, and egg.

Lay one tube crescent roll dough along bottom of a 9 x 13-inch pan. Press to form a crust sealing cracks. Layer half the meat mixture, cottage cheese mixture, then remaining meat mixture. Sprinkle mozzarella cheese over top. Lay the remaining dough over the top, covering as much as possible. Bake 25 minutes, or until golden brown. Makes 6–8 servings.

CREAMY TORTILLA PIE

1 pound **ground beef**
1 **medium onion,** chopped
1 can (4 ounces) **diced green chiles,** with liquid
2 cans (8 ounces each) **tomato sauce**
1 envelope **taco seasoning**
4 **large flour tortillas**
3/4 cup **milk**
1 can (10.5 ounces) **cream of chicken soup,** condensed
2 cups **grated cheddar cheese,** divided

Preheat oven to 350 degrees.

In a frying pan, brown ground beef and onion together until meat is no longer pink. Drain if necessary. Stir green chiles, tomato sauce, and taco seasoning into meat mixture.

Center 2 large tortillas over two greased pie pans. Press tortillas down to form bottom crust. Evenly divide meat mixture between pans. Lay remaining tortillas over tops, cutting to fit if necessary.

In a bowl, combine milk and condensed soup. Pour half the soup mixture evenly over each pie. Sprinkle 1 cup cheese over top. Cover with aluminum foil and bake 15 minutes. Uncover and bake an additional 5 minutes, or until cheese melts. Makes 6–8 servings.

*One pie can be frozen to be used at a later date. Place the pie in the refrigerator 24 hours before baking. Bake thawed pie, covered in aluminum foil, at 350 degrees for 20 minutes. Uncover and bake an additional 5 minutes, or until cheese melts.

GRANDMA'S STUFFED BELL PEPPERS

6 **green bell peppers**
1 pound **ground beef**
1 **medium onion,** chopped
1 can (14.5 ounces) **Italian-style diced tomatoes,** with liquid
3/4 cup **uncooked instant white rice**
1 1/4 cups **water,** divided
1/3 cup **seasoned breadcrumbs**

Preheat oven to 350 degrees.

Bring a large pot of salted water to a boil. Cut the tops off the bell peppers. Remove seeds. Parboil the peppers in boiling water for 5 minutes. Carefully remove peppers and drain any excess water.

In a frying pan, brown ground beef and onion until meat is no longer pink. Drain if necessary. Stir in the tomatoes, rice, and water. Cover, and simmer over medium heat for 5 minutes, or until rice is tender. Remove from heat. Salt and pepper to taste. Stuff each pepper with beef and rice mixture. Place stuffed peppers open side up in a baking dish. Sprinkle tops with breadcrumbs. Pour 1/2 cup water in bottom of baking dish. Cover with aluminum foil and bake 30 minutes, or until heated through. Makes 6 servings.

AUNT LEARA'S ZUCCHINI BOATS

3 **medium zucchini**
1 pound **ground beef**
1 **medium onion,** chopped
1 can (8 ounces) **tomato sauce**
1 1/2 teaspoons **Italian seasoning**
salt
1 1/2 cups **grated mozzarella cheese**

Preheat oven to 350 degrees.

Peel zucchini. Cut in half length-wise and then scoop out seeds to form a boat.

Bring a large pot of salted water to a boil. Boil zucchini for 5 minutes. Remove zucchini and drain. Place in bottom of a 9 x 13-inch pan.

In a frying pan, brown ground beef and onion until meat is no longer pink. Stir in tomato sauce and Italian seasoning. Salt to taste. Fill zucchini with meat mixture. Sprinkle cheese evenly over top. Bake 20 minutes, or until heated through and cheese melts. Makes 4–6 servings.

MEXICAN PIZZA

2 teaspoons	**cornmeal**
1 loaf (1 pound)	**frozen bread dough,** thawed*
1/2 to 1 pound	**ground beef**
1	**small onion,** chopped
2 to 3	**cloves garlic,** minced
1 can (16 ounces)	**refried beans**
1 cup	**medium salsa**
1 can (4 ounces)	**chopped green chiles**
2 teaspoons	**chili powder**
1 to 2 cups	**grated Monterey Jack cheese**
2	**tomatoes,** diced
1 to 2 cups	**shredded or torn lettuce**

Preheat oven to 425 degrees.

Spray a 12-inch pizza pan or 8 1/2 x 11-inch pan with nonstick cooking spray. Lightly sprinkle cornmeal on sprayed pan, covering well. Roll dough on counter to fit bottom of pan. Place prepared dough in pan and then prick with fork all over. Bake for 10–12 minutes, or until lightly browned. Remove from oven and set aside.

In a large frying pan, brown ground beef, onion, and garlic. Drain if necessary. Combine refried beans, salsa, green chiles, chili powder, and cheese with cooked beef and heat through. Spread meat mixture over crust and return to oven for 5–7 minutes. Remove from oven and sprinkle with tomatoes and lettuce. Makes 4–6 servings.

*To thaw bread dough, place loaf on plate and cover with plastic wrap that has been sprayed with nonstick cooking spray. Place plate in refrigerator 24 hours before preparing recipe.

SAUCY TACOS

1 pound	**ground beef**
1	**medium onion,** chopped
1 can (8 ounces)	**tomato sauce**
1 envelope	**taco seasoning**
1 package	**hard or soft taco shells**
	shredded lettuce
	grated cheddar cheese
	salsa
	sliced olives
	sour cream

In a large frying pan, brown ground beef and onion until meat is no longer pink. Stir in tomato sauce and taco seasoning. Simmer over low heat for 5 minutes. Serve meat mixture in individual taco shells. Garnish with lettuce, cheese, salsa, olives, and sour cream. Makes 6–8 servings.

KIDS' FAVORITE LASAGNA

1 pound **ground beef**
1 1/2 teaspoons **Italian seasoning**
1 container (16 ounces) **cottage cheese**
1 **egg,** beaten
2 cups **grated mozzarella cheese,** divided
3/4 cup **water, divided**
2 jars (26 ounces each) **spaghetti sauce,** any variety
1 box (12 ounces) **oven-ready lasagna noodles,** uncooked

Preheat oven to 350 degrees.

In a frying pan, brown ground beef until no longer pink. Season with Italian seasoning.

In a bowl, combine cottage cheese, egg, and 1 cup mozzarella cheese.

Add 1/2 cup water and all but 1 cup of spaghetti sauce to beef. Spread reserved spaghetti sauce into bottom of a greased 9 x 13-inch pan. Layer 5–6 lasagna noodles over sauce, overlapping or breaking to fit, if necessary. Spread half the cheese mixture over noodles. Spoon a third of the beef mixture over cheese layer. Repeat layers once. Add one more layer of 5–6 noodles and spoon remaining beef mixture over top. Drizzle remaining water over top. Cover with aluminum foil and bake 50 minutes. Uncover and sprinkle remaining cheese over top. Bake, uncovered, 5 minutes more. Let stand 5 minutes before serving. Makes 8 servings.

VARIATION: 1 package (3.5 ounces) pepperoni can be added to the layers.

STUFFED MANICOTTI

1 pound	**ground beef**
1 package (8 ounces)	**manicotti pasta**
1 jar (26 ounces)	**spaghetti sauce,** divided
1 container (16 ounces)	**cottage cheese**
2 cups	**grated mozzarella cheese,** divided
1/2 cup	**grated Parmesan cheese**
1	**egg,** beaten
1 teaspoon	**dried oregano**

Preheat oven to 350 degrees.

In a frying pan, brown ground beef until no longer pink. Drain if necessary. Allow meat to cool.

Cook pasta according to package directions; drain and set noodles aside.

Pour approximately 1 cup spaghetti sauce into a greased 9 x 13-inch pan. Spread the sauce to cover the bottom of the pan. Stir cottage cheese, 1 cup mozzarella cheese, Parmesan cheese, egg, and oregano into warm meat. Stuff manicotti with meat mixture. Lay stuffed pasta in the pan. Spread remaining spaghetti sauce over stuffed shells. Sprinkle cheese over top. Cover with aluminum foil and bake 40 minutes. Uncover and bake an additional 5–10 minutes. Makes 6–8 servings.

*Use a cake decorating bag or a plastic sandwich bag with the corner cut off to pipe the manicotti filling into the pasta.

DRINDA'S BEEF STROGANOFF

1 pound	**ground beef**
1	**large onion,** chopped
4	**large carrots,** thinly sliced
1 can (4 ounces)	**sliced mushrooms,** liquid reserved
1 teaspoon	**minced garlic**
2 tablespoons	**vegetable oil**
3/4 teaspoon	**salt**
1/4 teaspoon	**pepper**
2 teaspoons	**paprika**
1/3 cup	**water**
3/4 cup	**sour cream**
1 package (12–16 ounces)	**hot cooked wide egg noodles**

In a large frying pan, brown ground beef and onion until meat is no longer pink.

In a separate pan, saute carrots, mushrooms, and garlic in oil until cooked through. Add vegetables, salt, pepper, paprika, mushroom liquid, and water to beef mixture. Cover and simmer slowly for 30 minutes. Stir in the sour cream and simmer for 3–4 minutes, or until heated through. Serve over hot noodles. Makes 4–6 servings.

MAGNIFICENT MEATBALLS

2 pounds	**ground beef**
1/2 cup	**breadcrumbs**
1	**egg**
1/4 cup	**finely chopped onion**
1/2 cup	**milk**
1/2 to 1 teaspoon	**salt**
1/2 teaspoon	**black pepper**
1/2 teaspoon	**oregano**
1/4 teaspoon	**anise seed**
1/4 teaspoon	**chili powder**
1 can (10.75 ounces)	**cream of mushroom soup,** condensed
1 soup can	**water**
1 package (12–16 ounces)	**hot cooked egg noodles**

Preheat oven to 350 degrees.

In a large bowl, combine all ingredients, except soup, water, and noodles. Mix well. Shape into 30–40 meatballs. Place meatballs on a 15 x 10 x 1-inch pan. Bake for 12–17 minutes, or until lightly browned. Transfer meatballs to a 2-quart baking dish.

In a small bowl, combine soup and water. Pour over meatballs. Cover and bake for 45 minutes to 1 hour, or until meatballs are no longer pink. Serve over hot cooked noodles. Makes 8–10 servings.

TACO PIE

1 (9-inch)	**deep-dish frozen piecrust,** thawed
1/2 pound	**ground beef**
1/2 envelope	**taco seasoning**
1/2 cup	**grated cheddar or Mexican-blend cheese**
1/2 cup	**crushed nacho-flavored chips**
1	**tomato,** diced
1 1/2 cups	**shredded lettuce**
	sour cream
	sliced black olives (optional)

Bake piecrust according to package directions until golden.

In a frying pan, brown ground beef until no longer pink. Season with taco seasoning. Spread cooked meat into bottom of baked piecrust. Layer cheese, chips, tomato, and lettuce over pie. Garnish with a dollop of sour cream and sprinkle olives over the top, if desired. Serve immediately. Makes 4–6 servings.

SWEET AND SOUR MEATBALLS

1	**egg**
1 cup	**breadcrumbs**
2 to 3	**cloves garlic,** minced
1/2 teaspoon	**salt**
1/4 teaspoon	**pepper**
2 pounds	**ground beef**
2 teaspoons	**vegetable oil**
1 cup	**chicken broth**
2	**large green bell peppers,** cut into chunks
2 cans (8 ounces each)	**unsweetened pineapple tidbits,** juice reserved
1/2 cup	**sugar**
3 tablespoons	**cornstarch**
1/2 cup	**cider vinegar**
2 to 3 tablespoons	**soy sauce**
8 cups	**hot cooked rice**

In a bowl, combine egg, breadcrumbs, garlic, salt, and pepper. Break up ground beef over egg mixture and combine well. Shape mixture into 30–40 meatballs.

In a frying pan, brown meatballs in oil. Add broth, bell peppers, and pineapple to meatballs. Bring to a boil. Reduce heat and simmer for 5–7 minutes.

In a separate bowl, combine sugar, cornstarch, vinegar, soy sauce, and reserved pineapple juice until smooth. Pour over meatballs. Bring to a boil, reduce heat and simmer for 2 minutes, stirring constantly. Serve over hot cooked rice. Makes 6–8 servings.

QUICK TAMALE PIE

1 pound	**ground beef**
1 can (14.75 ounces)	**cream-style corn**
1 envelope	**taco seasoning**
1 can (3.8 ounces)	**sliced olives,** drained
1 package (6.5 ounces)	**cornbread mix**
	ingredients used in mix

Preheat oven to 400 degrees.

In a large frying pan, brown ground beef until no longer pink. Stir in corn and taco seasoning. Spoon meat mixture into a greased deep-dish pie pan. Sprinkle olives over meat. Prepare cornbread batter according to package directions. Spread batter evenly over top. Bake for 15–17 minutes, or until golden brown. Makes 4–6 servings.

NOTES

NOTES

NOTES

NOTES

NOTES

NOTES

101 Things To Do With A Cake Mix

101 More Things To Do With A Cake Mix

101 Things To Do With A Slow Cooker

101 More Things To Do With A Slow Cooker

101 Things To Do With A Potato

101 Things To Do With A BBQ

101 Things To Do With A Tortilla

101 Things To Do With Ramen Noodles

101 Things To Do With A Casserole

101 Things To Do With A Dutch Oven

101 Things To Do With A Salad

101 Things To Do With Yogurt

101 Things To Do With Grits

ABOUT THE AUTHORS

Stephanie Ashcraft, author of the original *101 Things To Do With A Cake Mix*, was raised near Kirklin, Indiana. She received a bachelor's degree in family science and a teaching certificate from Brigham Young University. Since 1998, she has taught cooking classes based on the tips and meals in her cookbooks. She currently lives in Tucson, Arizona.

Janet Eyring's interest in learning how to cook healthy, inexpensive meals without living in the kitchen has inspired her many creative recipes. She also teaches cooking classes at Macey's Little Cooking Theatre. She is the co-author of several 101 series cookbooks. She currently lives in Highland, Utah.